SOCCER
MATH ON THE FIELD

BY TOM ROBINSON

Published by The Child's World®
1980 Lookout Drive • Mankato, MN 56003-1705
800-599-READ • www.childsworld.com

Acknowledgments
The Child's World®: Mary Berendes, Publishing Director
The Design Lab: Design and production
Red Line Editorial: Editorial direction

Photographs ©: Andreas Gradin/Shutterstock Images,
cover, title; Herbert Kratk/Shutterstock Images, 4–5;
Shutterstock Images, 6–7; The Design Lab, 9; Tim De
Waele/AP Images, 10–11; Hussein Malla/AP Images,
12–13; Photo Work/Shutterstock Images, 15; Michael
Dwyer/AP Images, 16; Shizuo Kambayashi/AP Images,
19; George Holland/AP Images, 21; Christof Stache/
AP Images, 22–23; Chris O'Meara/AP Images, 24;
AP Images, 27; David Bernal/isiphotos.com/Corbis/AP
Images, 29

ISBN 9781614734116
LCCN 2012946508

Printed in the United States of America
Mankato, MN
November, 2012
PA02144

ABOUT THE AUTHOR

Tom Robinson is the author of 33 books, including 25 about sports. The Susquehanna, Pennsylvania, native is an award-winning sportswriter and former newspaper sports editor.

TABLE OF CONTENTS

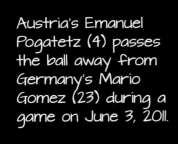

Austria's Emanuel Pogatetz (4) passes the ball away from Germany's Mario Gomez (23) during a game on June 3, 2011.

MATH ON THE FIELD

Soccer players run in long spurts down the field. It is a big part of the sport. Area shows how much space there is on the field. Players also consider angles when setting up shots.

Statistics are used to track games and seasons. Some soccer leagues use formulas to rank teams in the **standings**. **Percentages** and **averages** help compare goalkeepers.

There are many interesting and fun ways to look at the math of the game. Use your math skills as you take a look at soccer. You'll be surprised at how much they are needed!

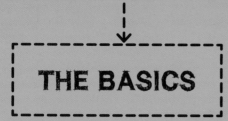
The Field

Soccer is known as football in many countries. The Federation Internationale de Football Association (FIFA) governs international soccer. FIFA rules state that fields can vary in length from 100 to 130 yards long by 50 to 100 yards wide.

For international play, FIFA allows larger fields that are 120 by 80 yards. But FIFA also allows fields as small as 110 by 70 yards.

In the United States, soccer is sometimes played on American football fields. Those fields are 120 yards long and 53 1/3 yards wide. On the youth level, soccer can be played on even smaller fields. Many youth leagues play with fewer than 11 players on a team so that each player can be more involved. At that level, having many different field sizes makes sense. For pro and international players, soccer is best played on wide fields. Skilled players spread the field and pass to move the ball.

Olympic Stadium in Kyiv, Ukraine

115 yards

What are the area and perimeter of the smallest FIFA international fields? How about for the largest FIFA international fields?

Area = length x width
110 x 70 = 7,700 square yards
120 x 80 = 9,600 square yards

The area of the smallest field is 7,700 square yards. The area of the largest field is 9,600 square yards.

Perimeter = (width x 2) + (length x 2)
110 x 2 = 220
70 x 2 = 140
220 + 140 = 360 yards

What is the perimeter of the largest field?
120 x 2 = 240
80 x 2 = 160
240 + 160 = 400 yards

The perimeter of the smallest field is 360 yards. The perimeter of the largest field is 400 yards.

74 yards

Covering Ground

Coach Diaz prepares his team for international play. He decides the formation he wants. Coach Diaz thinks about who best fits each position. He decides how much ground each player should cover. The players' speed and strength help him decide. The coach draws the field. The drawing shows the parts of the field that each player will cover.

Coach Diaz sets up a 4–4–2 grouping. He has four defenders covering equal space. He has four midfielders in a diamond shape. Two are on the outsides. Two are in the middle; one plays closer to the defenders.

Coach Diaz figures square yards for each player to cover. His team will play on a 120- by 80-yard field. The **penalty area** is 18 by 44 yards.

Here is what the coach found:

POSITION(S)	RESPONSIBILITIES	LENGTH (YARDS)	WIDTH (YARDS)	AREA (SQUARE YARDS)
Defenders	The defensive half of the field; width divided equally among the four.	60	20	1,200
Left midfield, Right midfield	The area between each penalty box; the space between the edge of the penalty area and the sideline.	84	18	1,512
Offensive midfield, Defensive midfield	From the goal line on one end to a spot midway between the penalty area and midfield on the other end; the width of the penalty area.	81	44	3,564
Left forward, Right forward	The offensive half of the field; width divided in half.	60	40	2,400

For defenders, the coach took half of the length of the whole field.

120 ÷ 2 = 60 yards

The coach then split the width of the field four ways.

80 ÷ 4 = 20 yards

He then multiplied the length by the width.

60 x 20 = 1,200

The defenders need to cover 1,200 square yards.

The offensive and defensive midfielders are asked to cover the most ground. Each has to cover all 60 yards on one end of the field.

These midfielders also need to cover 21 yards on the other end. That is halfway to the penalty area.

60 - 18 (penalty area width) = 42
42 ÷ 2 = 21
60 + 21 = 81 yards in length

The midfielders must cover a total of 81 yards in length.

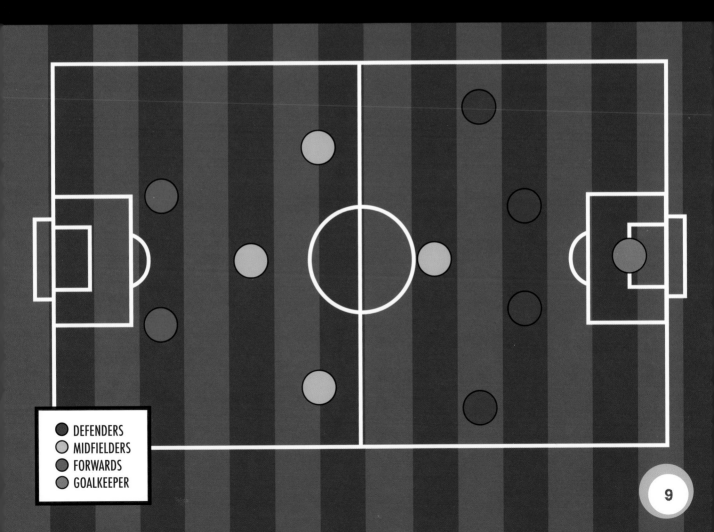

- DEFENDERS
- MIDFIELDERS
- FORWARDS
- GOALKEEPER

Scoring Angles

David Beckham scored all the way from midfield for Manchester United in a 1996 game against Wimbledon. The shot was one of many that made Beckham stand out as a player. It was selected as Goal of the Decade in the first ten years of the Premier League. Other players scored more often, but Beckham was one of the game's top threats to score off a free kick.

The best scorers in soccer are able to make the ball curve in flight. They strike it in a way that adds a sideways spin. They control the height, too. Sometimes they can put a shot over a goalie's head. This usually happens when the goalie moves toward the shooter. In turn, goalies try to be in the best spot to block the shooting area. For example, a player moves toward the corner. Then a goalie stands near the post to block out almost the entire shooting area.

There are different kinds of shooting angles. Angles are made from two rays that start from the same point. They are measured in degrees of a circle. A complete circle is 360°. Half of a circle is 180°. A quarter of a circle is 90°. The diagram shows some of the angles a player can use to shoot the ball into the goal.

As a player moves out from directly in front of the goal, the shooting angle gets smaller. A goalkeeper tries to move along the same angle, so he or she covers as much of the goal as possible.

David Beckham of England hits a free kick during the 2002 World Cup.

Penalty Kicks

Canada led the United States 3–2 late in a 2012 Olympic women's soccer semifinal game. The United States was awarded a **penalty kick**. As Abby Wambach waited to take the kick, the impact was clear. The United States had a great chance to tie the game. Wambach scored. The United States went on to win, 4–3.

Penalty kicks are given for two reasons in soccer. A penalty kick is awarded when a defensive player commits a foul inside the penalty box. Wambach's shot came because a Canada player touched the ball with her hand in the penalty box. On a penalty kick, a player is given a shot against the goalie from 12 yards away. The player stands directly in front of the middle of the goal.

Soccer also turns to penalty kicks to break ties in games. Sometimes there needs to be a winner, such as in playoffs and championship events. If the game is still tied after the extra time periods, a penalty kick **shootout** happens. Each team is given five penalty kicks to start.

The goalie has a large space to cover. A soccer goal is 24 feet from post to post and 8 feet high.

What is the area of the goal?

The distance between posts is length. The width is the shorter distance. It is from the crossbar to the ground.

$$24 \times 8 = 192$$

The goalie has an area of 192 square feet to defend.

Canada goalie Erin Mcleod (18) tries to stop a penalty kick by Abby Wambach (14) of the United States during the 2012 Olympics on August 6, 2012.

Soccer players are much more successful on their penalty kicks than hockey players are in on their penalty shots. The National Hockey League (NHL) uses shootouts if a regular-season game is tied after overtime. In 2011–12, NHL players made just 409 of their 1,209 penalty-shot attempts.

What percentage is that? Percentage tells how many times out of 100 an event occurs. To find the percentage, divide the goals by the attempts. Then multiply the number by 100.

$$409 \div 1{,}209 = 0.338 \qquad 0.338 \times 100 = 33.8$$

The NHL players scored on 33.8 percent of their penalty-shot attempts.

A bar graph compares the penalty kick success rate for Major League Soccer (MLS) with the penalty shot success rate in NHL shootouts. In the 2011 season, MLS shooters were 74-for-89 on their penalty kick attempts.

$$74 \div 89 = .831 \qquad .831 \times 100 = 83.1$$

The shooters made 83.1 percent of their penalty-kick attempts.

PENALTY SHOT SUCCESS

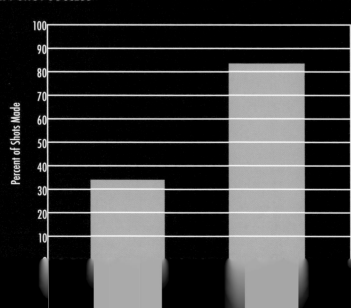

Eduardo Lillingston takes a penalty kick during the Chivas USA vs. Houston Dynamo match on October 25, 2009.

Sporting Kansas City players block a free kick by the New England Revolution in the second half of a game on April 23, 2011.

Standings

Sporting Kansas City finished the 2011 MLS season in style. The team won three times and tied twice in its final five games to finish first in its conference. Many soccer leagues and tournaments have standings that give three points for a win, one point for a tie, and no points for a loss.

As a low-scoring game, soccer games are often tied. Use a formula to find standings points. Points are equal to wins times three plus ties. Wins are multiplied by three because each win is worth three points.

standings points = (3 x number of wins) + ties
The 2011 results were:

TEAM	WINS	LOSSES	TIES
Sporting Kansas City	13	9	12
Houston Dynamo	12	9	13
Philadelphia Union	11	8	15
Columbus Crew	13	13	8
New York Red Bulls	10	8	16
Chicago Fire	9	9	16
D.C. United	9	13	12
Toronto FC	6	13	15
New England Revolution	5	16	13

Find the standings points for Sporting Kansas City.

3 x 13 (wins) = 39

39 + 12 (ties) = 51

Sporting Kansas City had 51 points in the standings.

What were Toronto FC's points?

3 x 6 = 18

18 + 15 = 33

Toronto FC had 33 points in the standings.

Scoring

Elon and Coastal Carolina were tied in their 2011 National Collegiate Athletic Association (NCAA) Tournament game. Then Ashton Bennett took over for Coastal Carolina. With just under eight minutes left, Coastal Carolina's Petro Ribeiro headed the ball toward Elon's goal. Then Bennett used his body to deflect the ball into the net. Bennett's goal sent Coastal Carolina to the next round with a 4–3 win. The junior showed why he was the top scorer in the country.

The NCAA ranks scorers by points per game. Players receive two points for goals and one for **assists**.

How do you find points per game averages?

Points per game average = [(2 x goals) + assists] ÷ games played

Bennett led the men's Division I scorers during the 2011 season. He had 23 goals and 7 assists in 22 games. What was his points per game average?

2 x 23 (goals) = 46

46 + 7 (assists) = 53

53 ÷ 22 (games played) = 2.41

Bennett had an average of 2.41 points per game.

The top women's scorers in Division I for 2011 are listed in order of goals scored. Find the points averages.

Player	School	Games	Goals	Assists	Points	Average
Maya Hayes	Penn State	26	31	8	70	2.69
Sarah Hagen	Milwaukee	21	26	9	61	
Rachel Tejada	Illinois State	19	21	9	51	
Morgan Marlborough	Nebraska	18	20	6	46	
Silvia Fuentes	Arkansas-Little Rock	21	15	28	58	

To find the average, divide the points by the games.

What was Sarah Hagen's average?

61 ÷ 21 = 2.90

Hagen averaged 2.90 points per game.

Rachel Tejada averaged 2.68 points.

51 ÷ 19 = 2.68

Morgan Marlborough averaged 2.56 and Silvia Fuentes 2.76 points.

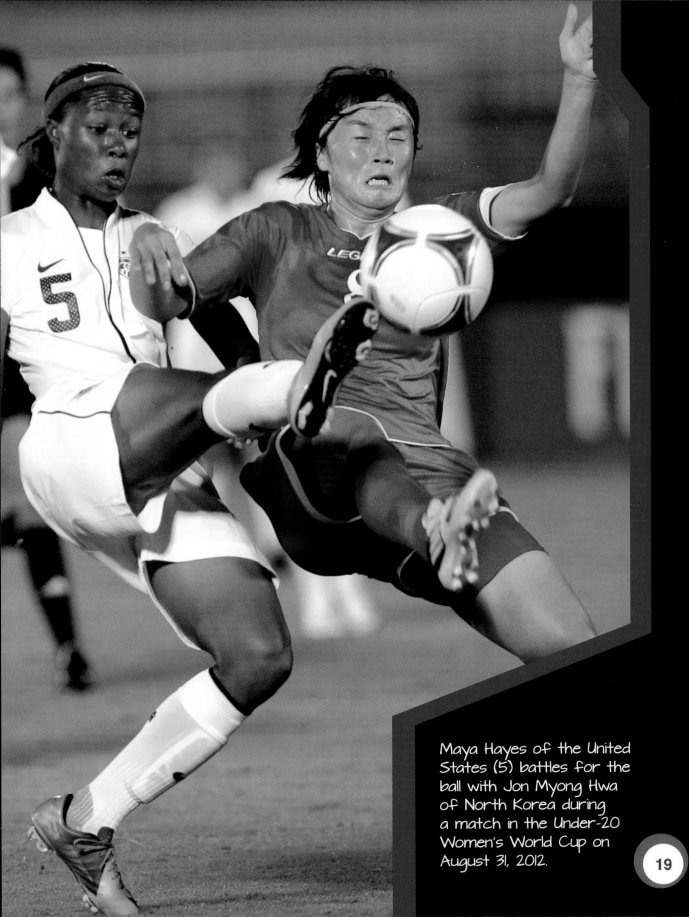

Maya Hayes of the United States (5) battles for the ball with Jon Myong Hwa of North Korea during a match in the Under-20 Women's World Cup on August 31, 2012.

Goals-against Average

Tally Hall had eight shutouts for the Houston Dynamo in the 2011 MLS season. A shutout is when a goalie plays the entire game without the other team scoring. Hall was strong game after game, as shown by his goals-against average.

The average can easily be found if a goalie has played in all complete games. Divide the goals allowed by the number of games.

Four goalies in MLS during 2011 all played every second of each of their games.

Tally Hall played all 3,420 minutes in the 38 games he played for Houston. Matt Pickens played 37 full games for Colorado. Kasey Keller of Seattle and Nick Rimando of Real Salt Lake both played 36 full games.

What were the players' goals-against averages?

Hall gave up 43 goals in 38 games.

$43 \div 38 = 1.13$

Hall had a 1.13 goals-against average.

Pickens gave up 45 goals in 37 games.

$45 \div 37 = 1.22$

Pickens had a 1.22 goals-against average.

Keller gave up 40 goals in 36 games.

$40 \div 36 = 1.11$

Keller's goals-against average was 1.11.

Rimando gave up 41 goals in 36 games.

$41 \div 36 = 1.14$

He had a 1.14 goals-against average.

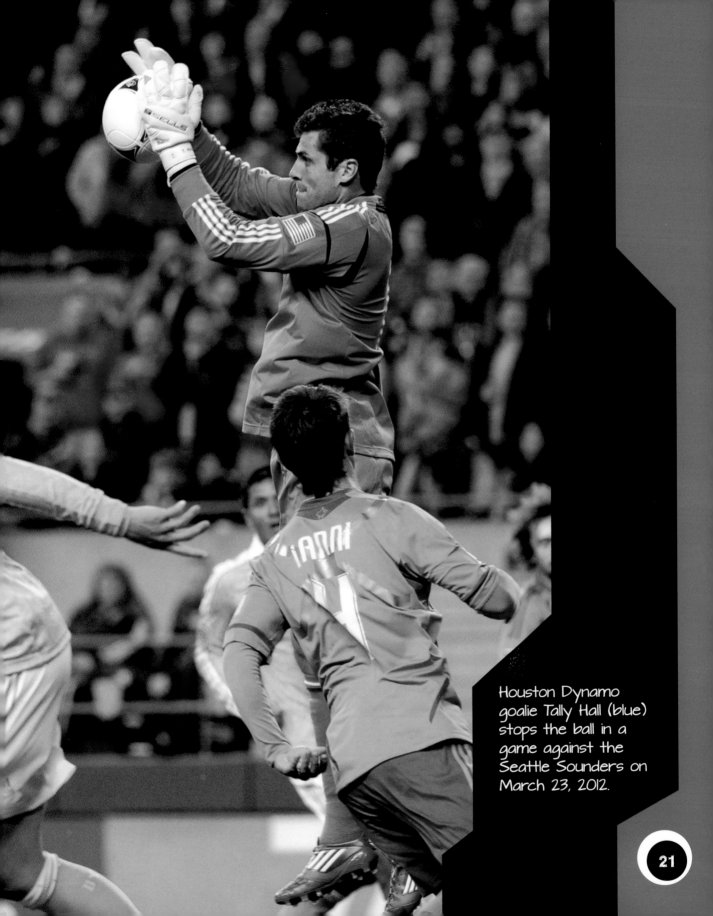

Houston Dynamo goalie Tally Hall (blue) stops the ball in a game against the Seattle Sounders on March 23, 2012.

AN INTERNATIONAL GAME

The World Cup

The World Cup is an international championship played by national teams. It was held for the first time in 1930 and again in 1934 and 1938. After a break during World War II (1939–1945), the World Cup resumed in 1950. It has been held every four years since.

The countries that have won two or more men's World Cup titles through 2010 are shown in this bar graph:

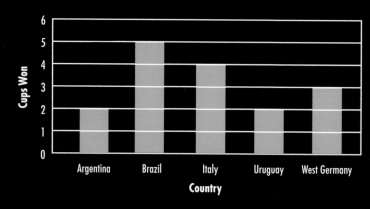

MEN'S WORLD CUP TITLES

Which country has the most titles? Which countries have won three championships?

The graph shows that Brazil has the most titles with five. Italy won four times. West Germany won three. Argentina and Uruguay each won twice.

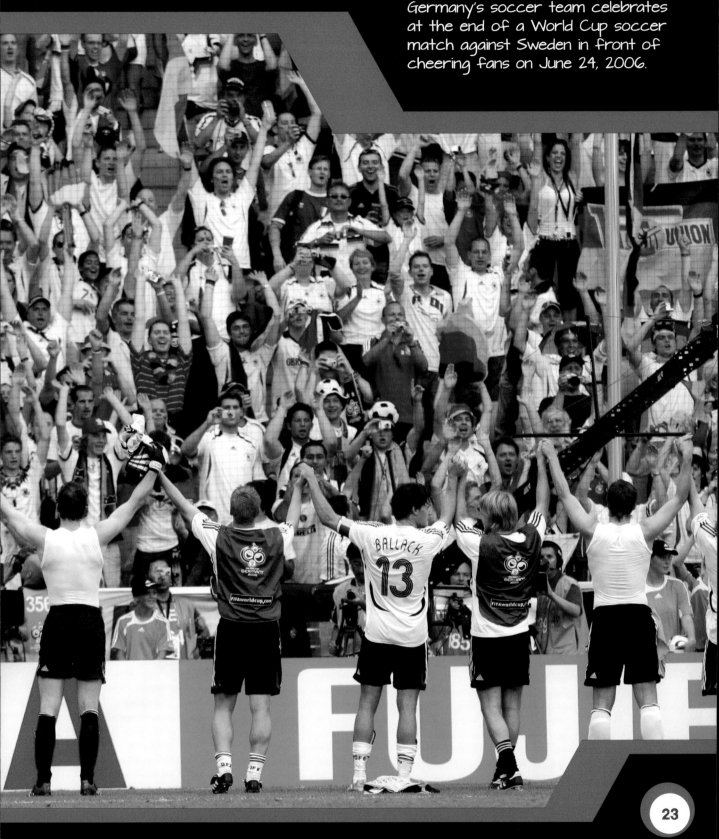

Germany's soccer team celebrates at the end of a World Cup soccer match against Sweden in front of cheering fans on June 24, 2006.

Mia Hamm (9) of the United States runs with her defender from Sweden during action in Olympic women's soccer on July 23, 1996.

Team USA Women

A total of 11 players have scored at least 100 points in the history of the U.S. Women's National Team. Mia Hamm scored a record 158 goals before retiring in 2004. Abby Wambach is second to Hamm. Wambach scored five times in the London 2012 Olympic Games, giving her 143 goals. Hamm and Wambach are first and third in career points scored. Kristine Lilly ranks second in points.

The top scorers in team history, through the end of 2012 Olympics were:

PLAYER	YEARS	GAMES	GOALS	ASSISTS	POINTS	AVERAGE POINTS PER GAME
Mia Hamm	1987–2004	275	158	144	460	1.67
Kristine Lilly	1987–2010	352	130	105	365	1.04
Abby Wambach*	2001–2012	188	143	59	345	1.84
Tiffeny Milbrett	1991–2005	204	100	61	261	1.28
Michelle Akers	1985–2000	153	105	36	246	1.61
Cindy Parlow	1996–2004	158	75	35	185	1.17
Shannon MacMillan	1993–2005	176	60	50	170	0.97
Carin Gabarra	1987–1996	117	53	47	153	1.31
Julie Foudy	1988–2004	272	45	55	145	0.53
Tisha Venturini	1992–2000	132	44	21	109	0.83
Heather O'Reilly*	2002–2012	170	34	38	106	0.62

*Active as of 2012

Which players had more assists than goals? Julie Foudy and Heather O'Reilly had more assists than goals. Hamm and Lilly are the only players with more than 100 goals and 100 assists.

Which player had the highest average points per game? Wambach's 1.84 was the highest average.

Career Path

Pele is a Brazilian star who came to the United States to play late in his career. He is widely regarded as soccer's all-time greatest scorer. Counting goals for his pro teams and Brazil, Pele had 1,281 from 1956 to 1977. Pele's career included helping Brazil win three World Cup titles in 1958, 1962, and 1970. Pele also helped boost the popularity of soccer in the United States. He played for the New York Cosmos of the North American Soccer League from 1975 to 1977.

This line graph shows Pele's 77 career goals for Brazil through the years.

PELE'S GOALS FOR BRAZIL

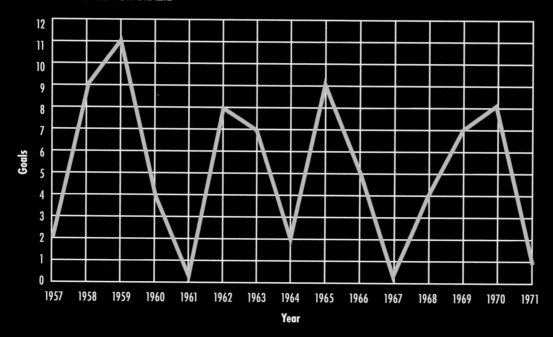

Which year did Pele score the most goals? How many did he score that year? During which year did Pele score his 50th career goal for Brazil?

The highest-scoring year was 1959 when he had 11 goals. The 50th goal of Pele's career with Brazil came during 1965.

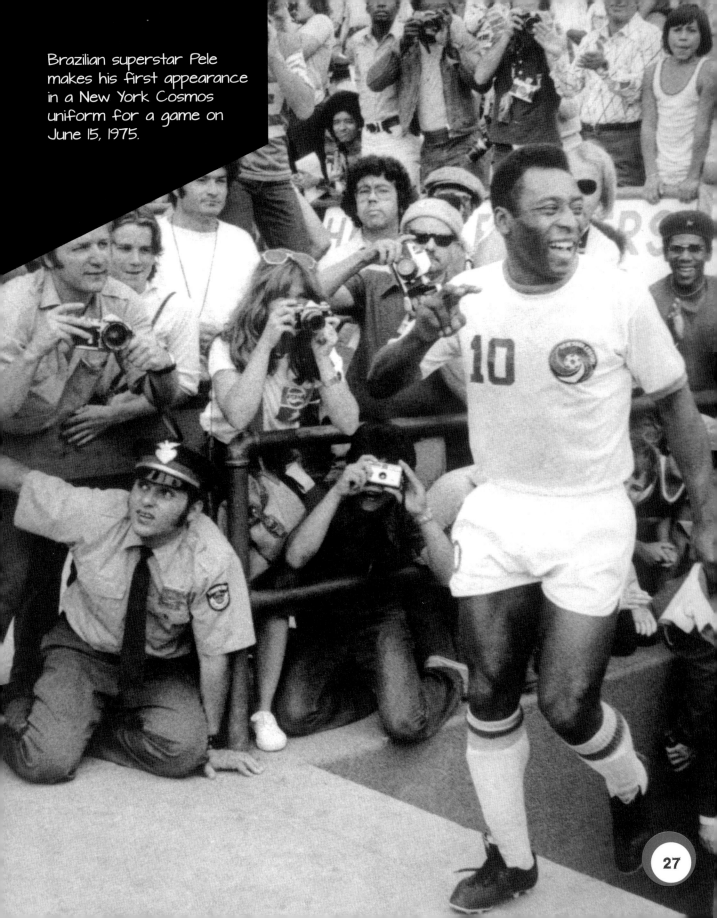

Brazilian superstar Pele makes his first appearance in a New York Cosmos uniform for a game on June 15, 1975.

1. At the end of a season, a soccer team has 12 wins and nine ties. The standings give three points for a win and one point for a tie. What are the team's standings points?

2. Goalie Josh Saunders made 11 saves and allowed two goals for the Los Angeles Galaxy in the 2011 MLS playoffs. What percentage of the shots did Saunders save?

3. A goalie is only allowed to use his or her hands in the penalty box. The penalty box is 44 yards by 18 yards. How big is the area in which the goalie can use his hands?

Answer Key

1. $12 \times 3 = 36$
   $9 \times 1 = 9$
   $36 + 9 = $ **45 standings points**

2. $11 + 2 = 13$ total shots
   $11 \div 13 = .846$
   $.846 \times 100 = $ **84.6 percent**

3. $44 \times 18 = $ **792 square yards**

Josh Saunders of the Los Angeles Galaxy jumps to make a save during a game against the New England Revolution on March 31, 2012.

29

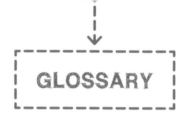

assists (uh-SISSTS): Assists are passes that set up goals. College players receive one point for assists.

averages (AV-uh-rij-iz): Averages are found by adding up a group of figures and then dividing the total by the number of figures added. Points averages are found by dividing the points by the games.

extra time (EK-stra TIME): Extra time is time that is added to a game that is tied. If the game is still tied after extra time, it might go to a penalty kick shootout.

penalty area (PEN-uhl-tee AIR-ee-uh): Penalty areas are at the ends of a soccer field, and are the only areas in which the goalies can handle the ball. Fouls in the penalty areas lead to penalty kicks.

penalty kick (PEN-uhl-tee KIK): A penalty kick is when a shooter gets to shoot on goal without defenders from 12 yards away as the result of an opposing player committing a foul in the penalty box. A penalty kick shootout is often used to decide games that are tied after overtime.

percentages (pur-SEN-tij-iz): Percentages are numbers out of a hundred. The percentages of goals scored is greater in a soccer shootout than in a hockey shootout.

shootout (shoot-OWT): A shootout is a series of penalty kick attempts given to each team to break a tie in the game. A shootout happens if a game is still tied after extra time in a tournament.

standings (STAN-dingz): Standings are the positions or rankings of all teams within a league based upon their wins, ties, and losses. In soccer standings, a win counts for three points and a tie counts for one point.

statistics (stuh-TISS-tiks): Statistics are facts or pieces of information expressed in numbers or percentages. Statistics are used to track games and seasons.

LEARN MORE

Books

Mahaney, Ian F. *The Math of Soccer*. New York: PowerKids Press, 2012.

Minden, Cecilia, and Katie Marsico. *Soccer*. Ann Arbor, MI: Cherry Lake, 2009.

Woods, Mark, and Ruth Owen. *Goal!: Soccer Facts and Stats*. New York: Gareth Stevens, 2011.

Web Sites

Visit our Web site for links about soccer math:
childsworld.com/links

Note to Parents, Teachers, and Librarians: We routinely verify our Web links to make sure they are safe and active sites. So encourage your readers to check them out!

INDEX